BEHIND the BOOKCASE

Miep Gies, Anne Frank, and the Hiding Place

Barbara Lowell

illustrated by Valentina Toro

KAR-BEN
PUBLISHING

For Anna Myers, who makes dreams come true
—B.L.

To my family, for showing me the magic power of stories
—V.G.T.

KAR-BEN PUBLISHING®
An imprint of Lerner Publishing Group, Inc.
241 First Avenue North
Minneapolis, MN 55401 USA

Website address: www.karben.com

Main body text set in Johnston ITC Std Medium.
Typeface provided by International Typeface Corp.

Image credits: Paul Gies, pp. 38, 39.

Library of Congress Cataloging-in-Publication Data

Names: Lowell, Barbara, author. | Toro, Valentina, illustrator.
Title: Behind the bookcase : Miep Gies, Anne Frank, and the hiding place /
    Barbara Lowell ; illustrated by Valentina Toro.
Description: Minneapolis : Kar-Ben Publishing, 2020. | Series: Holocaust |
    Audience: Ages 7–11 | Audience: Grades 2–3 | Summary: "Miep Gies, who as
    a girl was a refugee during World War I, recognized that the world had once
    again become a dark place. Especially in danger were Jewish people during
    the Nazi occupation of the Netherlands, like her boss's family. This is the
    story of how Miep helped hide the Frank family." —Provided by publisher.
Identifiers: LCCN 2019028761 | ISBN 9781541557253 (library binding) | ISBN
    9781541557260 (paperback)
Subjects: LCSH: Gies, Miep, 1909–2010—Juvenile literature. | Righteous
    Gentiles in the Holocaust—Netherlands—Amsterdam—Biography—Juvenile
    literature. | Frank, Anne, 1929–1945—Juvenile literature. | Jewish children in
    the Holocaust—Netherlands—Amsterdam—Juvenile literature. | Holocaust,
    Jewish (1939–1945)—Netherlands—Amsterdam—Juvenile literature.
Classification: LCC DS135.N6 G545 2020 | DDC 940.53/18092 [B]—dc23

LC record available at https://lccn.loc.gov/2019028761

Manufactured in the United States of America
1-46141-45746-2/14/2020

When the world was a very dark place, Miep Gies helped hide Anne Frank.

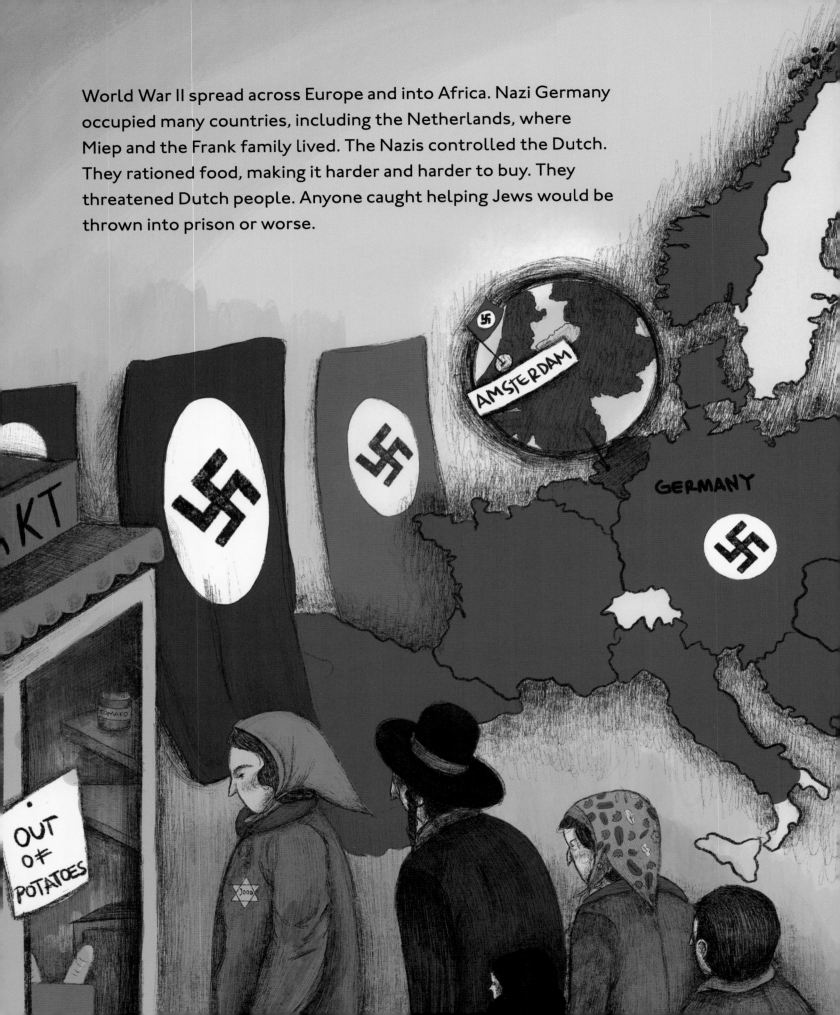

World War II spread across Europe and into Africa. Nazi Germany occupied many countries, including the Netherlands, where Miep and the Frank family lived. The Nazis controlled the Dutch. They rationed food, making it harder and harder to buy. They threatened Dutch people. Anyone caught helping Jews would be thrown into prison or worse.

The Nazis forced Jewish people to wear a yellow star on their coats that said "Jood," the Dutch word for Jew. They stole the Dutch Jews' possessions, homes, and freedom.

Miep worked for Otto Frank. He and his family were Jewish. Their lives had become unpredictable and dangerous under Nazi occupation.

Mr. Frank called Miep into his office. He told her that he planned to hide his family in the empty rooms above the offices. He asked Miep for help. They both knew the danger if they were caught.

Miep said yes without hesitating.

Some of Mr. Frank's other employees—Mr. Koophuis, Mr. Kraler, and his secretary, Elli Vossen—would help too.

Miep knew what war meant.

World War I started when she was five. Miep had lived in Vienna, Austria, with her parents in an old, dark apartment. The Austrians, along with the Germans, lost the war.

Miep's family had little food. She grew weak and sick. She might have died, but the Dutch offered to care for Austria's children. Her parents sent her to the Netherlands when she was eleven.

Miep took a train to the Netherlands with other children. At the station in Leiden, the children sat in rows. Strings hung around their necks. Attached to the strings were cards in a language they could not read.

A man approached Miep. He picked up her card and read.

"Ja," he said and took Miep's hand.

At his house, his wife, a woman with soft eyes, welcomed Miep. Their children—four boys and a girl—lived there too. Instead of calling her by her Austrian name, they gave her the Dutch name, Miep, and showed her how to butter bread and sprinkle chocolate pieces on top. They called the chocolate pieces hailstones and mice. Miep had never tasted anything so delicious.

Miep learned to speak Dutch and moved to Amsterdam with her new foster family. When she grew up, she went to work for Mr. Frank. Where would World War II take the Frank family?

Not long after Mr. Frank talked to Miep, his sixteen-year-old daughter, Margot, received a notice. The Nazis ordered her to report to a German labor camp. It was time for the Franks to go into hiding.

Mr. Frank had not told his family where they would hide. But Miep knew. She led Margot to the office. They rode their bikes in the pouring rain. They were outlaws. Jews were forbidden to have bikes. Miep was forbidden to help Jewish people.

But there were no police outside to stop them. The police stayed inside because of the rain.

Soon Mr. and Mrs. Frank and their thirteen-year-old daughter, Anne, appeared at the office door. They wore layers of soaking-wet clothes because they could not be seen carrying suitcases.

Miep helped them up the narrow stairs of the hiding place and closed the door behind them.

Later, when no one would be in the office, Miep
visited them. She was amazed to see boxes and sacks
of food, pots and pans, and furniture scattered about.
She had no idea when Mr. Frank had brought it all.

Anne and Mr. Frank dashed around putting everything into place.
But Mrs. Frank and Margot sat on a bed and seemed lost.

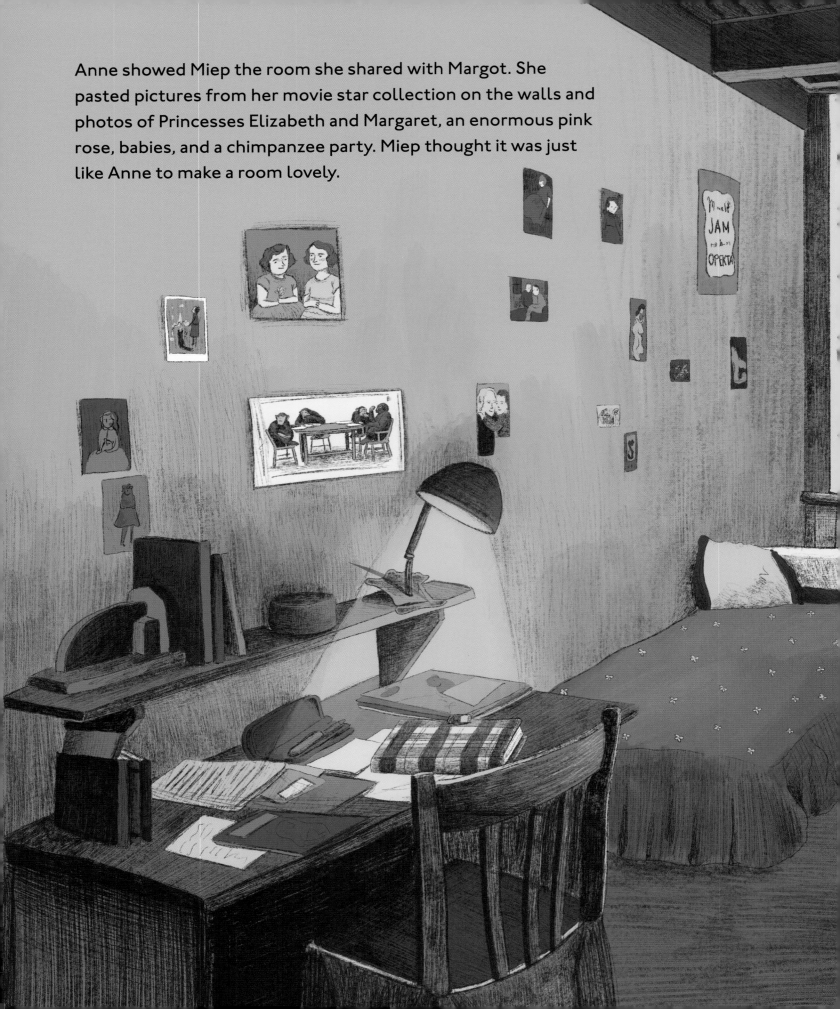

Anne showed Miep the room she shared with Margot. She pasted pictures from her movie star collection on the walls and photos of Princesses Elizabeth and Margaret, an enormous pink rose, babies, and a chimpanzee party. Miep thought it was just like Anne to make a room lovely.

Miep visited the Franks every morning. Anne greeted Miep first and asked for the latest news.

One morning, Miep told the family that the darkest days had come. The Nazis had rounded up many Jews and sent them away to labor and concentration camps.

Anne asked about her friends. But Miep did not know. Trying to find out was dangerous. Without girlfriends to share secrets with, Anne wrote her secrets in the diary she called Kitty.

More people joined the Franks in the hiding place—Mr. van Daan and his wife; their son, Peter; and Miep's dentist, Dr. Dussel. A bookcase was hung on hinges to conceal the door to the hiding place.

Miep wanted to be available to all of them but especially to Anne. She knew how it felt to be young and leave everything in your world behind. Miep listened to her concerns. She answered Anne's many questions. They talked about boys, fashion, and makeup—things Anne was curious about.

Miep decided to buy something special for Anne. She searched all over Amsterdam before finding a pair of used, red high heels. Anne slipped her feet inside and wobbled a bit at first, but soon she pranced back and forth across the floor. It was a small moment of happiness in their dark world.

Anne asked if Miep and her husband, Henk, could spend the night. Henk worked for the Dutch Resistance and would never reveal their secret.

So one night, Miep and Henk stayed in the hiding place. The Westertoren church clock chimed every fifteen minutes. Anne thought of the clock as a friend because it broke the silence. But Miep could not sleep listening to it chime. She began to feel the same fear her friends felt every day. The hours passed. In the morning, Miep knew how it felt to be a Jew in hiding.

Miep and everyone in the hiding place lived from day to
day hoping that the war would soon end. It continued.
Miep became like a hunter searching for food. Somehow,
she always found something for everyone to eat even if it
was half-rotten. Everyone became thin. Their clothes were
dirty from lack of soap. They were cold and had little coal to
burn that second winter. Would the war never end?

Then June 6, 1944, brought real hope. D-Day! The Allied forces invaded Nazi-occupied France. Help was coming!

But it seemed to take so long.

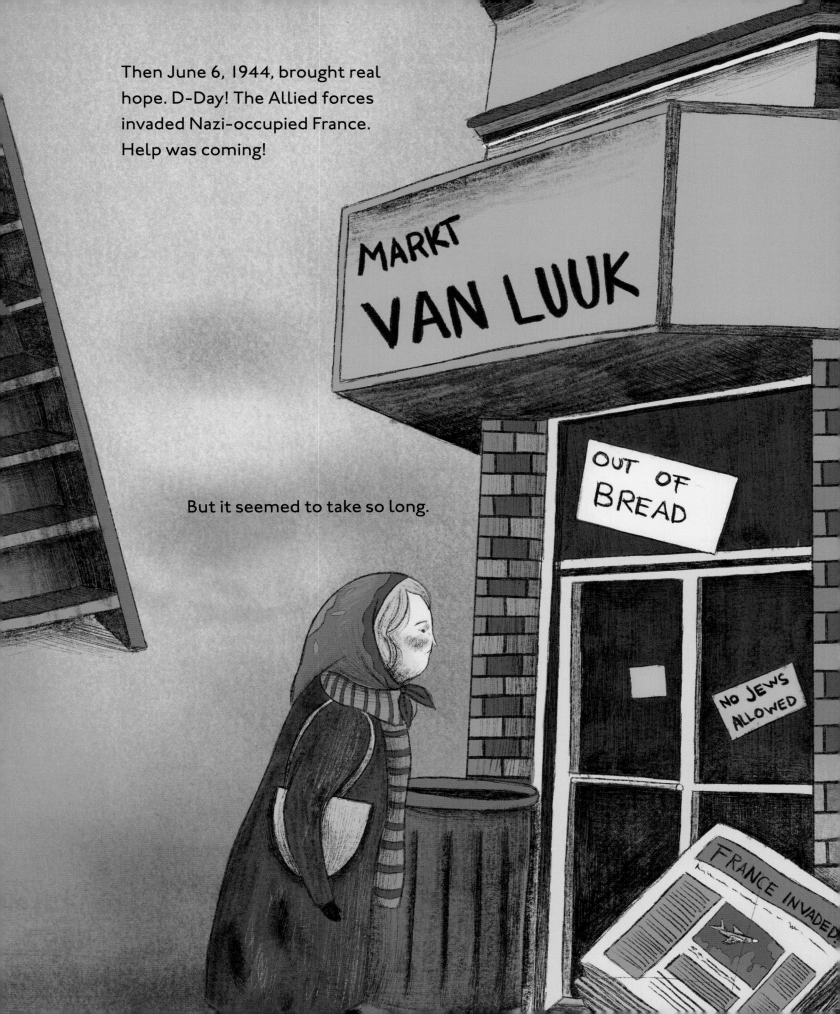

One day, a Nazi officer entered the office.
He told Mr. Frank's secretary, Elli, and Miep
to stay put and not to move.

They were terrified. Someone had betrayed
Anne and the others in hiding.

Miep heard their footsteps coming down the stairs for the first time in two years. Then they were gone. Everything Miep and the others had done to keep them safe had failed.

Henk appeared at the office door. He had seen the Franks and the van Daans and Dr. Dussel taken away in a police truck. Elli, Henk, and Miep hurried upstairs to save whatever they could. They knew the Nazis would return.

Miep spotted Anne's diary on the floor. She did not open it. She did not let anyone read it.

Miep kept the diary safe for Anne.
But . . .

Anne did not return after the war ended.

Of all the people in the hiding place, only Mr. Frank returned from the concentration camps. Miep gave him Anne's diary. It comforted him.

When Mr. Frank published her diary, the world learned Anne's story. Miep was grateful that Anne's voice would still be heard. For many, Anne became the face of the Holocaust. In her diary, Anne wrote, "I want to go on living even after my death!"

Because Miep saved her diary, Anne's voice lives on. She lives in the hearts of readers who will always remember her.

"I am not a hero. I stand at the end of the long, long line of good Dutch people who did what I did or more. . . . Never a day goes by that I do not think of what happened then."
—Miep Gies

Author's Note

Twelve-year-old Miep (*right*) with members of her foster family, 1921.

I was inspired to write *Behind the Bookcase* after reading Miep Gies's book, *Anne Frank Remembered: The Story of the Woman Who Helped to Hide the Frank Family*, and visiting the Anne Frank House in Amsterdam. I wanted to tell the story to children of how this brave woman, Miep Gies, tried to save Anne Frank's life during the Holocaust and how saving her diary allowed others to hear Anne's story.

In her diary, Anne Frank changed the names of the people she mentioned. Miep Gies used the same names in her book. I have also used these names, but I added their actual names in parentheses here.

Born Hermine Santrouschitz, Miep, suffering from malnutrition after World War I, was sent to the Netherlands. When she was sixteen, she visited her Austrian family in Vienna. Miep loved living in Amsterdam and wanted to stay there. Her parents gave Miep permission to continue living with her Dutch family, the Nieuwenhuises.

In 1933, the Franks moved from Frankfurt, Germany, to Amsterdam to escape Nazi oppression under the newly elected German chancellor, Adolph Hitler. Mr. Frank opened the Dutch Opekta Company, which manufactured pectin for making jam. He soon hired Miep. She became close friends with fellow employee, Elli Vossen (Elizabeth "Bep" Voskuijl), and the Franks.

In 1938, the Nazis began their conquest of Europe that led to World War II. On May 10, 1940, the Nazis invaded the Netherlands and soon occupied the country. Oppression of Jewish citizens began immediately and steadily increased. That July, Miep married Henk Gies (Jan Gies). In December, Otto Frank moved his company to a larger location at 263 Prinsengracht. The building housed an annex, an additional space above the offices that had been used for storage. A bookcase was hung on hinges to conceal the entrance once the annex was used as a place to hide. Mr. Frank continued to run the Opekta Company but gave legal control to employees Mr. Koophuis (Johannes Kleiman) and Mr. Kraler (Victor Kugler). He believed having non-Jewish control would be safer for the company and its employees.

Under Nazi occupation, Anne Frank and her family's freedom was strictly limited. They could not own bicycles, ride streetcars, go to the movies, shop at non-Jewish stores, or attend non-Jewish schools. Jews were forced to register with the authorities and were easily identified by the yellow star they wore on their coats. Mr. Frank and his Jewish business partner, Mr. van Daan (Hermann van Pels), realized that they would probably have to go into hiding at some point to prevent arrest by the Nazis. They prepared the annex by secretly stocking it with food, furniture, and other necessities.

On July 5, 1942, Mr. Frank received a notice demanding that Margot report to a German labor camp in nine days. The next day, the Franks went into hiding. Soon after, the Nazis began rounding up Jews and sending them to labor and death camps. The van Daan's (Hermann, Auguste, and Peter van Pels) followed the Franks into hiding a week later. After four months, Miep's dentist, Dr. Dussel (Fritz Pfeffer), joined them. Everyone in the annex had to be extremely quiet during the day. Many people went in and out of the offices below, and only five of the company's employees knew the secret. The people in hiding depended on Miep and the others for survival.

Victor Kugler, Bep Voskuijl, and Miep Gies (*front row*) at the Prinsengracht office, 1941.

During the war, the Nazis offered money for the location of Jews in hiding because of severe food shortages. An estimated 25,000 Jews in the Netherlands hid during the war, and 8,000 to 9,000 were discovered and arrested. On August 4, 1944, Anne Frank, her family, the van Daans, and Dr. Dussel were arrested along with Mr. Koophuis and Mr. Kraler. No one knows who betrayed them. The two employees were sent to a Dutch labor camp. Everyone else was first transported to Westerbork, a temporary camp in the Netherlands, before being sent to Auschwitz in Poland on September 3, 1944. They were on the last train from the Netherlands to Auschwitz.

The Nazi arresting officer, Karl Silberbauer, found Mr. Frank's briefcase, which held Anne's diary, notebooks, and papers. Silberbauer tossed the diary and the briefcase's contents on the floor. Miep found Anne's writings and kept them safe for her return. Miep was later grateful that she had not read the diary during the war, saying she would have burned it to protect the people mentioned.

Anne and Margot Frank were transferred from Auschwitz to a German labor camp, Bergen-Belsen, in October 1944. They died of typhus in February or March 1945, a short time before the camp was liberated.

Miep holds son Paul as Otto Frank (*left*) and Jan Gies look on, 1951.

Everyone who hid with Anne Frank died except Otto Frank. He was liberated from Auschwitz on January 27, 1945, and returned to Amsterdam four months later. When Otto Frank learned that Anne and Margot had died, Miep gave him Anne's diary. He published it in 1947. Miep read the diary after publication and said, "I was glad I'd read it at last. . . . So much had been lost, but now Anne's voice would never be lost."

Source Notes

36 Anne Frank, *Anne Frank: The Diary of a Young Girl* (New York: Modern Library, 1952), 211.

37 Miep Gies and Alison Leslie Gold. *Anne Frank Remembered: The Story of the Woman Who Helped to Hide the Frank Family* (New York: Simon & Schuster, 1987), 11.

39 Gies and Gold, 246.

Bibliography

Blair, Jon. *Anne Frank Remembered*. DVD. London: Jon Blair Film, 1995.

"The Diary at 70: Anne Frank Her Life and Her Legacy." *Life*, Volume 17, No. 9 (May 12, 2017).

Frank, Anne. *Anne Frank: The Diary of a Young Girl*. New York: Modern Library, 1952.

Gies, Miep, and Alison Leslie Gold. *Anne Frank Remembered: The Story of the Woman Who Helped to Hide the Frank Family*. New York: Simon & Schuster, 1987.

National Geographic. *Anne Frank's Holocaust*. DVD. Washington DC: National Geographic, 2015.

Pieter Van Huystee Film. *Otto Frank, Father of Anne*. DVD. Amsterdam: Pieter Van Huystee Film, 2010.

Van der Rol, Rudd, and Rian Verhoeven. *Anne Frank beyond the Diary*. New York: Viking, 1993.

Further Reading

BOOKS

Abramson, Ann. *Who Was Anne Frank?* New York: Penguin Workshops, 2007.

Dauvillier, Loic, Greg Salsedo, and Marc Lizano. *Hidden: A Child's Story of the Holocaust*. New York: First Second, 2014.

Gottisfeld, Jeff, and Peter McCarty. *The Tree in the Courtyard: Looking through Anne Frank's Window*. New York: Knopf Books for Young Readers, 2016.

Yolen, Jane. *Stone Angel*. New York: Philomel, 2015.

WEBSITES

Anne Frank House, http://www.annefrank.org

The Hiding Place, http://www.annefrank.org/en/Anne-Frank/secret-annex/

GREYSCALE

BIN TRAVELER FORM

Cut By _Juliet Evans_ Qty _42_ Date _28/10/24_

Scanned By_____ Qty_____Date_____

Scanned Batch IDs

_____   _____   _____

Notes / Exception

_____

_____

_____

_____

_____